PIANO | VOCAL | GUITAR

THE FRAY

SCARS & STORIES

W9-BUA-795

ISBN 978-1-4584-3472-2

HAL•LEONARD® CORPORATION
7777 W. BLUEMOUND RD. P.O. BOX 13819 MILWAUKEE, WI 53213

In Australia Contact:
Hal Leonard Australia Pty. Ltd.
4 Lentara Court
Cheltenham, Victoria, 3192 Australia
Email: ausadmin@halleonard.com.au

For all works contained herein:
Unauthorized copying, arranging, adapting, recording, Internet posting, public performance, or other distribution of the printed music in this publication is an infringement of copyright. Infringers are liable under the law.

Visit Hal Leonard Online at
www.halleonard.com

CONTENTS

4 HEARTBEAT

10 THE FIGHTER

18 TURN ME ON

23 RUN FOR YOUR LIFE

34 THE WIND

43 1961

50 I CAN BARELY SAY

56 MUNICH

63 HERE WE ARE

70 48 TO GO

79 RAINY ZURICH

84 BE STILL

HEARTBEAT

Words and Music by JOSEPH KING
and ISAAC SLADE

© 2011 EMI APRIL MUSIC INC., LITTLE BIKE MUSIC and LINCOLN & OLLIE MUSIC
All Rights Controlled and Administered by EMI APRIL MUSIC INC.
All Rights Reserved International Copyright Secured Used by Permission

F♯m D A
you got a fi - re and it's burn - ing in the rain. Thought
F♯m D A
that it went out, but it's burn - ing just the same. And you don't
F♯m A/D A E F♯m7 A/D
look back, not for an - y - thing, 'cause you love some - one, you love 'em all the same. If you love
E F♯m7 A/D
some - one, you love 'em all the same.
𝄋
F♯m A D
Oh, I'm feel - in' your

A
E/G♯
F♯m
A
D
heart - beat.
And, oh,
you're com - in' a - round,
A
E
F♯m
A
D
com - in' a - round,
com - in' a - round.
If you can love some - bod - y,
love 'em all the same.You got - ta
(D.S.) Vocal ad lib.
A
E/G♯
F♯m
A
D
To Coda
love some - bod - y,
love 'em all the same. I'm sing - in',
oh,
I'm feel - in' your
(D.S.) ad lib. ends

1
A
E
F♯m
D
A
heart - beat.
F♯m
D
A
I'm try'n' to
2
A
heart - beat.
Amaj7/E
C♯m7
4fr
Dmaj7
E/D
D(add2)
Ooh.

Dmaj7/A
E/A
D/A
Ooh.
I know the mem - o - ries rush - ing in - to your mind.

Dmaj7/E
E
D
Ooh.
I wan - na kiss your scars to - night.

A/E
D
I'm lay - ing here, 'cause you got - ta try, you got - ta let me in,

E
D
D.S. al Coda
let me in, now.
CODA
A
E
F♯m
A
D
heart - beat. Oh, your heart - beat. Yeah,
A
E
F♯m
A
D
I said, oh, your heart - beat. Yeah,
A
Amaj7/E
C♯m7
4fr
D
oh, your heart - beat.

THE FIGHTER

Words and Music by JOSEPH KING,
ISAAC SLADE, DAVID WELSH
and BEN WYSOCKI

© 2012 EMI APRIL MUSIC INC., LITTLE BIKE MUSIC, LINCOLN & OLLIE MUSIC, MOKOS MUSIC and POTALIAN PUBLISHING
All Rights for LITTLE BIKE MUSIC and LINCOLN & OLLIE MUSIC Controlled and Administered by EMI APRIL MUSIC INC.
All Rights Reserved International Copyright Secured Used by Permission

F
Just this one last time.
I swear you'll still be mine.
Gsus
3fr
But he can't pro-mise much.
Fmaj7/A
He
Csus
3fr
goes for one last touch,
one last touch.
F
Am
C
F
May-be we were meant to be lone-ly, lone-ly.
May-be we were meant to be on

Am
C
F
Am
C
our own.
Lone - li - ness has al - ways been with me, with me.
F
Am
C
To Coda
May - be we don't have to be all a - lone.
C5
3fr
C
The fight - er goes in - side, the
Am
dawn is creep - in' in.
He swings with all his might

C
Am
at all that mat - tered then. And
F
she's in love with him but lov - ers don't al - ways
G
Am
win. He nev - er ev - en saw the swing.
C
D.S. al Coda
She calls out his name, calls his name.

CODA
F
Am
F
C
G
F
Am
What breaks your bones
F
C
G
F
is not the load you're car - ry - in'. What breaks you down
Am
F
C
G
is all in how you car - ry.

Bm
Em
The lov - er held her love.
D
Gmaj7/B
She begs him not to go.
She un - wraps his gloves.
D
Gmaj7/B
The lov - er said, "I know, I know, I know."
G
Kissed his trem - b'ling lips,
she touched his fin - ger - tips.

Asus
Gmaj7/B
Some - how they both know
Dsus
G
he's not com - ing home, com - ing home.
Bm
D
G
Bm
D
G
Bm
D
G
Bm
D

G
Bm
D
G
Lone - li - ness has al - ways been with me, with me. May - be we were meant to be on
Bm
D
G
Bm
D
our own. What I got in - side of me will de - stroy me. So
G
Bm
D
G
may - be we don't have to be all a - lone.

TURN ME ON
(Burning)

Words and Music by JOSEPH KING,
ISAAC SLADE, DAVID WELSH
and BEN WYSOCKI

© 2012 EMI APRIL MUSIC INC., LITTLE BIKE MUSIC, LINCOLN & OLLIE MUSIC, MOKOS MUSIC and POTALIAN PUBLISHING
All Rights for LITTLE BIKE MUSIC and LINCOLN & OLLIE MUSIC Controlled and Administered by EMI APRIL MUSIC INC.
All Rights Reserved International Copyright Secured Used by Permission

Am
C
Fmaj7
back in my blood - line and we try to walk a - way.
- in' and you're fall - in' and I try to look a - way.
C
Am
C
But I want you as my lov - er. You are
But I'm fro - zen in the dark - ness, you're a
Fmaj7
C
F
where I wan - na stay.
burn - in' cab - ar - et.
And I don't know what it is, what it is,
Dm
what it is a - bout you. What it is, what it is but oh,

F
Am
Dm
the way you move - in'. Oh, you turn me on.
Am
F
Am
To Coda
I wan - na touch you 'til we're burn - in'. Oh,
1
Dm
C
Am
you turn me on.
C
Fmaj7
C
See you ris -

2
Dm
C
F
you turn me on. Come and turn me on.
G
Dm
C
F
G
Dm
C
F
Dm
D.S. al Coda
Oh,

CODA
Dm
C
you turn me on. Come and turn me on.
F
G
Dm
I wan - na feel, I wan - na feel you love. I wan - na feel, oh,
C
F
C/G
I said I wan - na feel. The way you're mov - in'. Oh,
Dm
C
F
you turn me on. Come and turn me on.

RUN FOR YOUR LIFE

Words and Music by JOSEPH KING
and ISAAC SLADE

© 2012 EMI APRIL MUSIC INC., LITTLE BIKE MUSIC and LINCOLN & OLLIE MUSIC
All Rights Controlled and Administered by EMI APRIL MUSIC INC.
All Rights Reserved International Copyright Secured Used by Permission

Fsus2
sis - ters with noth - ing be - tween; if one of us falls,
lay your bod - y down on the floor; you're des - p'rate to hear
Am
C
1
the oth - er will soon be fol - low -
her foot - steps a - gain. But this
Fsus2
ing."
Am
C

2
G(add4)
F
house is on fire, we need to go.
Am(add♭6)
Am
Csus
3fr
Whoa whoa, you don't have to
C
F
F(add2)
Dm7
go it a - lone, go it a - lone.
C
Run for your life, my love.

Gsus
3fr
Run and you don't give up. With
Fmaj7
Am7
all that you are, all that you want.
C
Gsus
3fr
I will be close be - hind.
N.C.
Run for your life.

Fsus2
She hac a fi - re in - side, and that ter - ri - fies
Am
C
you. You swore that you'd nev - er lose your con -
Fsus2
trol. Ba - by, let your - self go, 'cause
Am
C
part of you hides, and I know the hun - ger in -

G(add4)
side of you's strong. You can on - ly
F
hold back the riv - er so long.
Am(add♭6)
Am
Whoa, whoa,
Csus
3fr
C
F
you don't have to go it a - lone.

F(add2)
Dm7
Am(add♭6)
Whoa, whoa,
Am
Csus
3fr
C
you don't have to go it a - lone,
F
F(add2)
D
go it a - lone. Run for your life,
C
my love. Run and you don't

Gsus
3fr
give up. With all that you are,
Fmaj7
Am7
with all that you want. Run for your life
C
right now. And if you don't
C/E
To Coda
know how, I'll come back with you

Fmaj7
Am7
and take all that's true and leave all that's
C
G/B
burned be - hind. Run for your life.
Am
C
Whoa,
F
Dm7
whoa, you don't have to

Am
C
go it a - lone,

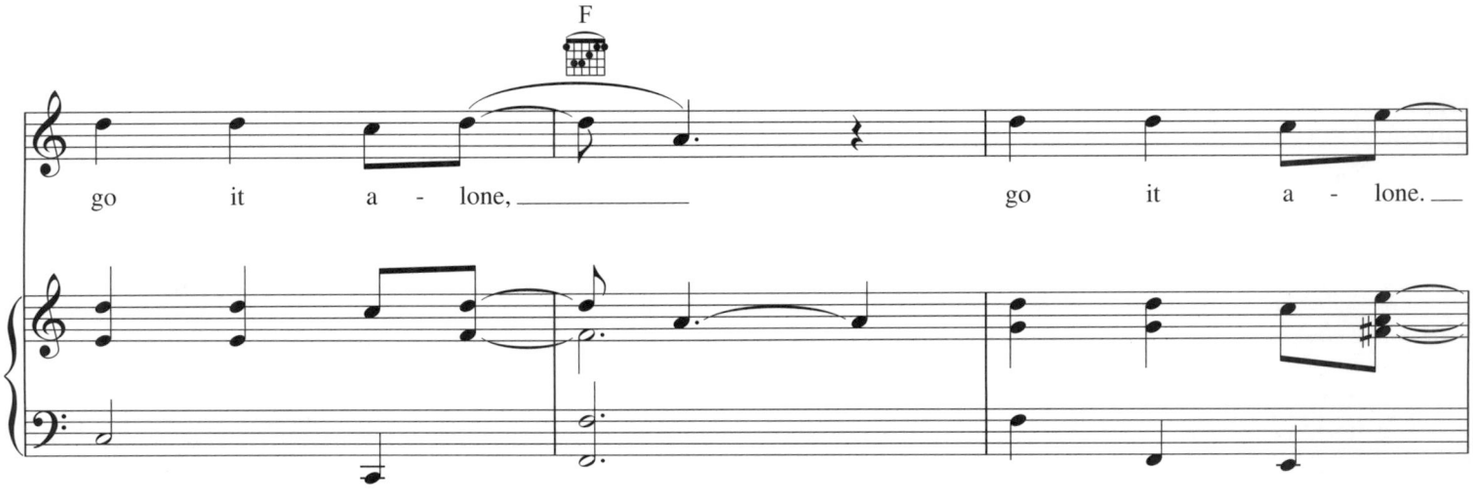
F
go it a - lone,
go it a - lone.

D
D.S. al Coda
Run for your life.

CODA
how,
I'll

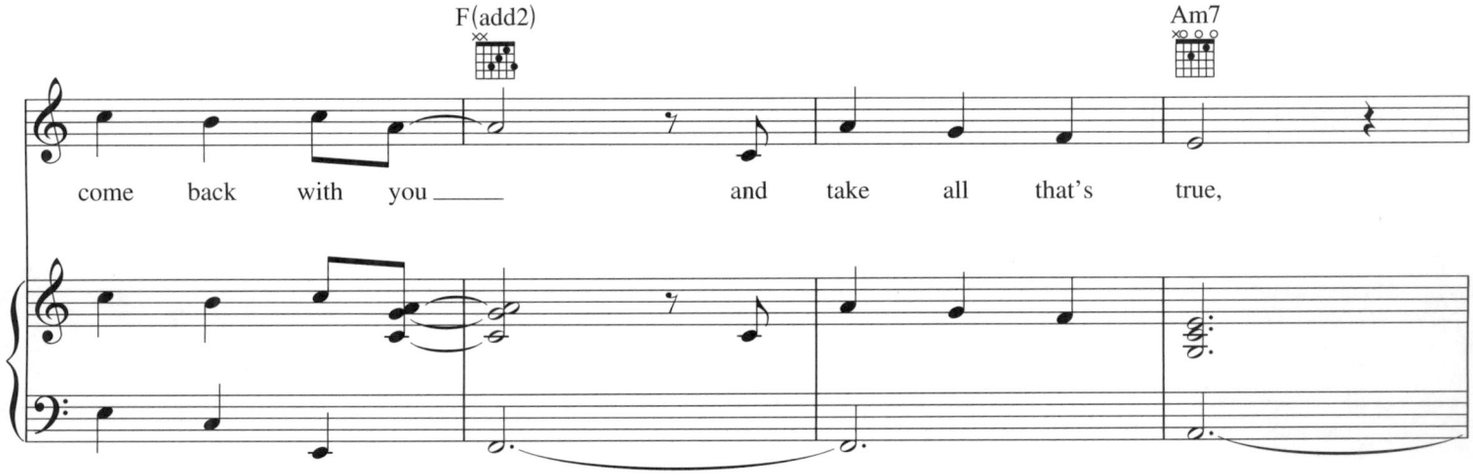
F(add2)
Am7
come back with you
and take all that's true,

C
G
leave al that's burned be - hind.
G(add4)
Fsus2
So run for your life.
Am
C
1
2
F
Run for your life.

THE WIND

Words and Music by JOSEPH KING,
ISAAC SLADE, DAVID WELSH
and BEN WYSOCKI

* *Recorded a half step lower.*

© 2012 EMI APRIL MUSIC INC., LITTLE BIKE MUSIC, LINCOLN & OLLIE MUSIC, MOKOS MUSIC and POTALIAN PUBLISHING
All Rights for LITTLE BIKE MUSIC and LINCOLN & OLLIE MUSIC Controlled and Administered by EMI APRIL MUSIC INC.
All Rights Reserved International Copyright Secured Used by Permission

Em
C
lost the land be - tween the sky and sea.
G
And I'm
Em/G
C/G
won - d'rin' will the wind ev - er come for me.
G
Yeah, 'cause I don't

Em
D
C
know, I don't know where I am.
Em
G
Can you tell me, will I break
D
C
Em
To Coda
or will I bend? Will the
D
C
G
wind ev - er come a - gain? Ooh,

C
G
ooh.
C
G
I
C/G
feel the sun com - in' out ris - in' from the east.

G
And I see the em - pire
C/G
fall - in' to her knees.
G
Ooh,
ooh. And I lost the line be - tween
Em/G
C/G
her and me.
G
Ooh,

Em/G
ooh. My trou - bles are gone if the wind
C/G
G
D.S. al Coda
ev - er comes for me. Yeah, 'cause I don't
CODA
D
C
Em
D
wind ev - er come? With you I've found the shore
C
Em
D
line. You were stand - ing there.

C
Em
D
And you I found you wait -
C
G/B
- ing. You were wait - ing for me, wait -
C
G
- ing for me.
Tried to kiss the emp - ti - ness.

Los_ the line be - tween sky and sea.
I feel the sun com - in' up, com - in' up,
com - in' up, com - in' up. And I don't
Em
D
C
Em
know, I don't know where I am. I will break

D C Em D C
or I will bend.
Will the wind ev - er come a - gain?
G C G
Yeah,
yeah,
C G C
yeah,
Em D C G
yeah.

1961

Words and Music by JOSEPH KING
and ISAAC SLADE

© 2012 EMI APRIL MUSIC INC., LITTLE BIKE MUSIC and LINCOLN & OLLIE MUSIC
All Rights Controlled and Administered by EMI APRIL MUSIC INC.
All Rights Reserved International Copyright Secured Used by Permission

A
F♯m
Some - one don't want us to - geth - er but we just keep on walk -
C♯m
4fr
A
- in' 'cause we're one.
Oh.
F♯m
C♯m/E
4fr
A
I got a voice and you
Third broth - er, nine -
F♯m
C♯m
4fr
got a rea - son.
- teen eigh - ty nine,
For the glo - ry we sing our bro - ken song.
got through it o - pened up the line.

A
F♯m
Take a side and I'll take the oth - er one. Two broth - ers un -
Stand tall, I'll fol - low you this time. We're all just wait -
C♯m
4fr
E
- der one na - tion.
- in' on a sign.
Wan - na feel your love
Dmaj7
E
right now. Wan - na see the night and feel the day.
Dmaj7
Ev - er try to touch some - bod - y nine - ty miles a - way?

E
F♯m
But it won't be the same
A
Dmaj7
a - gain.
(1., 2.) No, it
(D.S.) Can't go
F♯m
A
Dmaj7
To Coda
won't be the same a - gain.
back to the way it's been.
1
A
Yeah.

F♯m
C♯m
4fr
2
I'll be
F♯m
A
Dmaj7
with you un - til the end
F♯m
A
but it won't be the same. We're bro -
Dmaj7
Bm
F♯m
- ken, we're bat - tered. We're torn up and we're shat -

E
Dmaj7
Bm
- tered. We turn back on each oth - er the mo -
F♯m
E
Dmaj7
- ment that it mat - tered. The cur - tain is shak -
Bm
F♯m
E
- ing, it's bend - ing and it's break - ing. And I'll
Dmaj7
Bm
be with you in the end.

D.S. al Coda
But it
CODA
F♯m
I'll be with you un - til
A
Dmaj7
the end
but it
F♯m
E
won't be the same,
won't be the same
Dmaj7
a - gain.

I CAN BARELY SAY

Words and Music by JOSEPH KING
and ISAAC SLADE

© 2012 EMI APRIL MUSIC INC., LITTLE BIKE MUSIC and LINCOLN & OLLIE MUSIC
All Rights Controlled and Administered by EMI APRIL MUSIC INC.
All Rights Reserved International Copyright Secured Used by Permission

F6
C(add2)
but you can prob - 'ly tell;
a pow - der keg
if an - y - bod - y sees,
they'll turn,
E♭maj7
3fr
F6/9
Am
in a pris - on cell.
I wan - na re - turn,
they'll run from me.
D
Em(add2)
but all you will do is turn to leave.
Gmaj7/C
Am
D
B7/D♯
If I can find my way home,
will you take hold

Em
Csus2
3fr
of me?
'Cause I've been gone so
G5
3fr
G5/F♯
long, I can bare - ly say; all I know is,
Em7
Csus2
3fr
now I want to stay.
Has it been too
G5
3fr
G5/F♯
long since I went a - way? 'Cause I'm try'n' to

Em7
1
Csus2
3fr
G5
3fr
find the words, that I can bare - ly say.
F6
C(add2)
E♭maj7
3fr
F6/9
2
Csus2
3fr
Am
D
can bare - ly say. I want - ed to run; I want - ed to love
Em
Am
and be loved in re - turn. But will I ev - er get back?

D
B7/D♯
Em
Do I know too much to re - turn?
Csus2
3fr
G5
3fr
F6
C(add2)
E♭maj7
3fr
F6/9
I've been gone so
G5
3fr
G5/F♯
long, I can bare - ly say; all I know is, now

Em7
Csus2
3fr
I want to stay.
Has it been too
G5
3fr
G5/F♯
long since I went a - way?
'Cause I'm try'n' to find
Em7
C
Cm
3fr
G5
3fr
the words, but I can bare - ly say.
F6
C(add2)
E♭maj7
3fr
F6/9
G5
3fr
rit.

MUNICH

Words and Music by JOSEPH KING,
ISAAC SLADE, DAVIS WELSH
and BEN WYSOCKI

* *Recorded a half step higher.*

© 2012 EMI APRIL MUSIC INC., LITTLE BIKE MUSIC, LINCOLN & OLLIE MUSIC, MOKOS MUSIC and POTALIAN PUBLISHING
All Rights for LITTLE BIKE MUSIC and LINCOLN & OLLIE MUSIC Controlled and Administered by EMI APRIL MUSIC INC.
All Rights Reserved International Copyright Secured Used by Permission

let it go. In - side, the snow be -

gins to fall. Step to the edge, you and I, and we

fall be - low. Take a breath, hold my hand,

C5/B♭
5fr
and now you're not a - lone. Girl, you know,

C5
3fr
Dm7
it ter - ri - fies me, and I
F5
C5/B♭
5fr
don't know why. There you go,
C5
3fr
Dm7
you par - a - lyze me; and I
F5
F/A
B♭sus2
Gm7(add4)
C(add4)
Fsus2/A
don't know why. Ev - 'ry - thing is black and

Dm7
F5/E
F5
F/A
B♭sus2
Gm7(add4)
white and gray.
Walls are shak - ing
C(add4)
C(add4)/E
Dm7
F5/E
To Coda
when you're touch - ing me.
F5
F/A
B♭sus2
Gm7(add4)
C(add4)
Chang - es ev - 'ry - thing
when you're close to me.
F5
We're back to back,

N.C.
hand to hand, face to face a - gain; lov - ers and

en - e - mies, then we're back to friends. Some-thing left

hold - ing us pulls me clos - er in.

D.S. al Coda
Take a breath, and the col - or will re - turn a - gain.

CODA
F5
F/A
B♭sus2
Gm7(add4)
Chang - es ev - 'ry - thing,
C(add4)
A7♯5/C♯
4fr
Dm7
F5/E
chang - es ev - 'ry - thing.
F5
F/A
B♭sus2
Gm7(add4)
C(add4)
A7♯5/C♯
4fr
(Ah, ah, ah, ah, ah, ah.
Dm7
F5/E
F5
F/A
Ah, ah, ah, ah, ah, Walls are ah.

B♭sus2
Gm7(add4)
C(add4)
shak - ing; chang - es
Ah, ah, ah, ah, ah, ah.
Dm7
F5/E
F5
F/A
B♭sus2
Gm7(add4)
ev - 'ry - thing
Ah, ah, ah, ah, ah, ah. Ah, ah, ah.)
C(add4)
F5
when you're close to me.

HERE WE ARE

Words and Music by JOSEPH KING,
ISAAC SLADE, DAVID WELSH
and BEN WYSOCKI

© 20 2 EMI APRIL MUSIC INC , LITTLE BIKE MUSIC, LINCOLN & OLLIE MUSIC, MOKOS MUSIC and POTALIAN PUBLISHING
All Fights for LITTLE BIKE MUSIC and LINCOLN & OLLIE MUSIC Controlled and Administered by EMI APRIL MUSIC INC.
All Rights Reserved International Copyright Secured Used by Permission

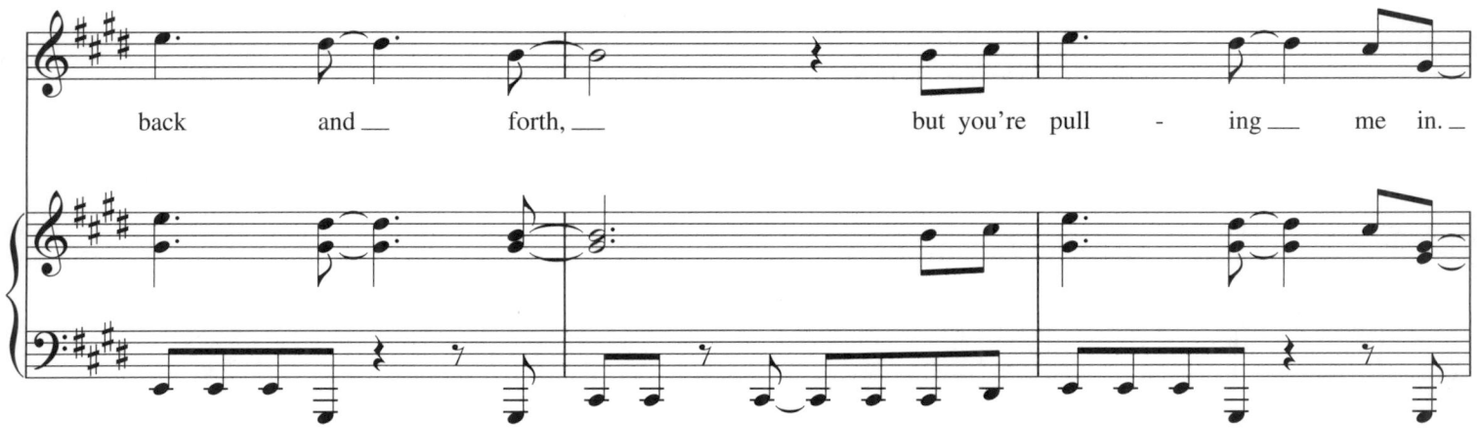
back and forth, but you're pull - ing me in.

I'm go - ing back and forth; show me

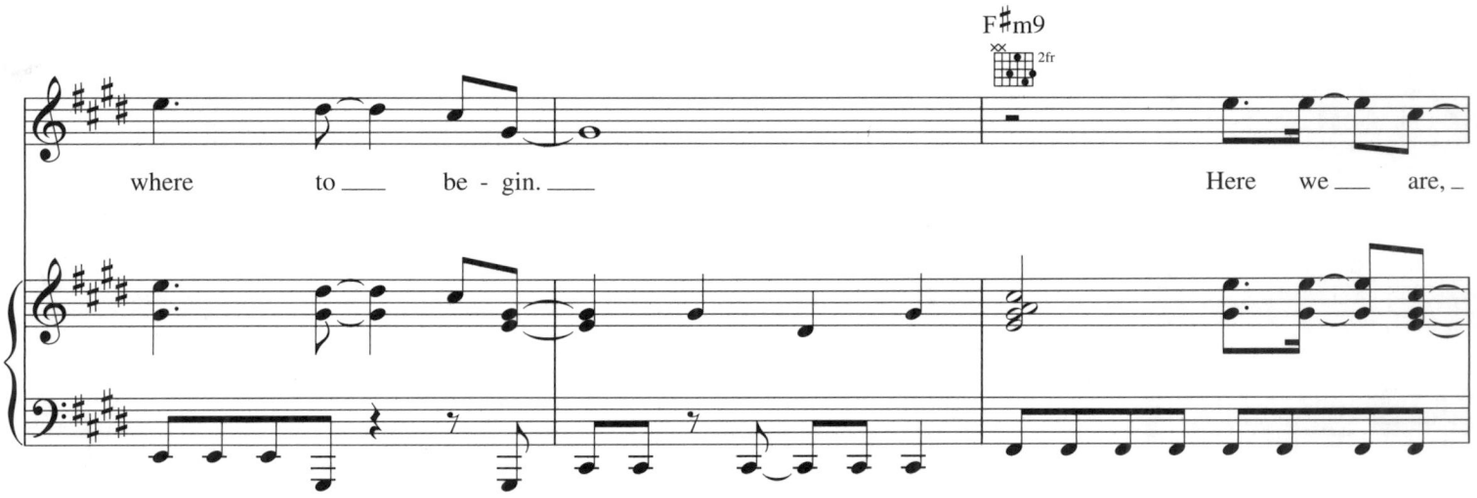
F♯m9
2fr
where to be - gin. Here we are,

𝄋
C♯m/E
4fr
C♯m7
4fr
B6
here we are, will you lay your bod - y down.

F♯m9
2fr
C♯m/E
4fr
C♯m7
4fr
Here we are, here we are, two
B6
Amaj7
F♯m7
lov - ers in the dark. Here we are, here we are,
E6
B6
To Coda
will you lay your bod - y, lay your bod - y down.
N.C.

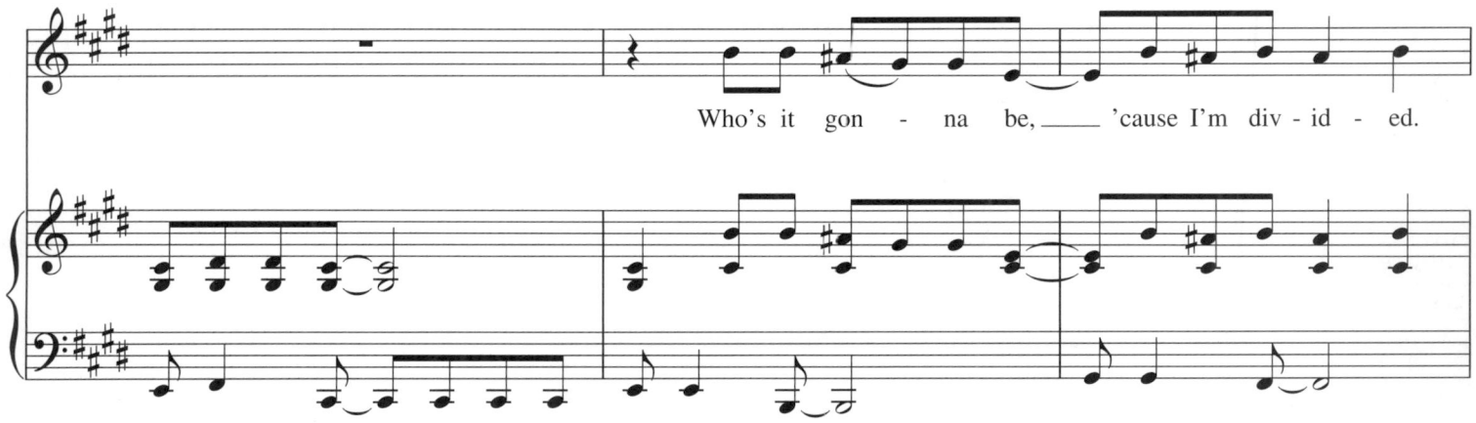
Who's it gon - na be, 'cause I'm div - id - ed.

Who you gon - na see? Have-n't de - cid - ed. Good - bye, hel - lo

to all the pres - sure; sev - en bil - lion hands up - on my shoul-ders, go - in',

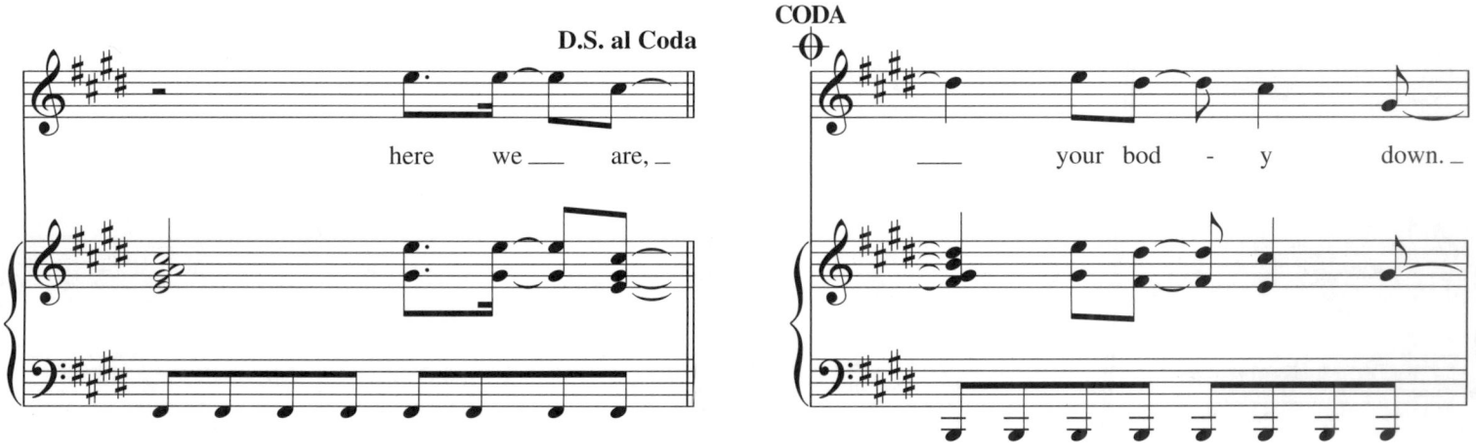
D.S. al Coda
here we are,
CODA
your bod - y down.

N.C.
Instrumental solo
I'm go - in' back and forth,
Solo ends
but you're pull - ing me in.
I'm go - ing

back and forth; show me where to be - gin.
F♯m9
C♯m/E
C♯m7
Here we are, here we are, will you lay
B6
F♯m9
C♯m/E
your bod - y down. Here we are, here we are,
C♯m7
B6
F♯m9
two lov - ers in the dark. Good - bye, hel - lo

C♯m/E
4fr
C♯m7
4fr
B6
to all the mad - ness;
sev - en bil - lion hands
up - on my shoul - ders, go - in',
Amaj7
F♯m7
E6
here we are,
here we are,
will you lay
B6
N.C.
your bod - y, lay
your bod - y down.

48 TO GO

Words and Music by JOSEPH KING,
ISAAC SLADE, DAVID WELSH
and BEN WYSOCKI

* *Recorded a half step higher.*

© 2012 EMI APRIL MUSIC INC., LITTLE BIKE MUSIC, LINCOLN & OLLIE MUSIC, MOKOS MUSIC and POTALIAN PUBLISHING
All Rights for LITTLE BIKE MUSIC and LINCOLN & OLLIE MUSIC Controlled and Administered by EMI APRIL MUSIC INC.
All Rights Reserved International Copyright Secured Used by Permission

F C Am Em/G
- i - for - nia, by ___ way of ___
F C Am Em/G
Mex - i - co. ___ We're _ lost and we're find -
Dm C Am G
- ing each oth - er, and we ___ may nev - er see __
F C Am G
___ the West ___ Coast, we ___ may nev - er see __

F
C
C
Cmaj7/G
the West Coast.
Fsus2
Fmaj7
C
Cmaj7/G
Fsus2
Fmaj7
Em
Am
We're tak - ing it slow,
Fmaj7
but for now, we're two down and for - ty -

C
Cmaj7/G
Fsus2
eight to go.
To Coda
Fmaj7
C
Cmaj7/G
Fsus2
Fmaj7
Am
Em/G
F
C
Missed an ex - it in Al - bu - quer - que,
Am
Em/G
F
C
but we don't seem to mind at all.

Am
Em/G
Dm
C
We pull o - ver; the sun is burn - ing, and we
Am
G
F
C
D.S. al Coda
lay down to feel the rain fall.
CODA
Fmaj7
Dm
The des - ert wind's
C
G
Dm
blow - ing your hair back, win - dow down,

C
G
Dm
town af - ter town.
Where will we be in
C
G
F(add2)
half a cen - tu - ry?
Two down and
Fmaj7
C
Cmaj7/G
for - ty - eight to go.
Fsus2
Fmaj7
C
Cmaj7/G
Fsus2

Fmaj7
Am
Em/G
F
The sun ris - es in Ber - nar - di -
C
Am
Em/G
F
- no some - time af - ter six a. - m.
C
Am
Em/G
We could take Twen - ty - sev - en up Old
Dm
C
Am
G
Can - yon Road. Some - times you win be - fore

F
C
Am
G
you run, some - times you win be - fore...
Fmaj9
We got
for - ty - eight,
for - ty - eight to go.
C
Cmaj7/G
Fsus2
Fmaj7
Lead Vocal continues ad lib.

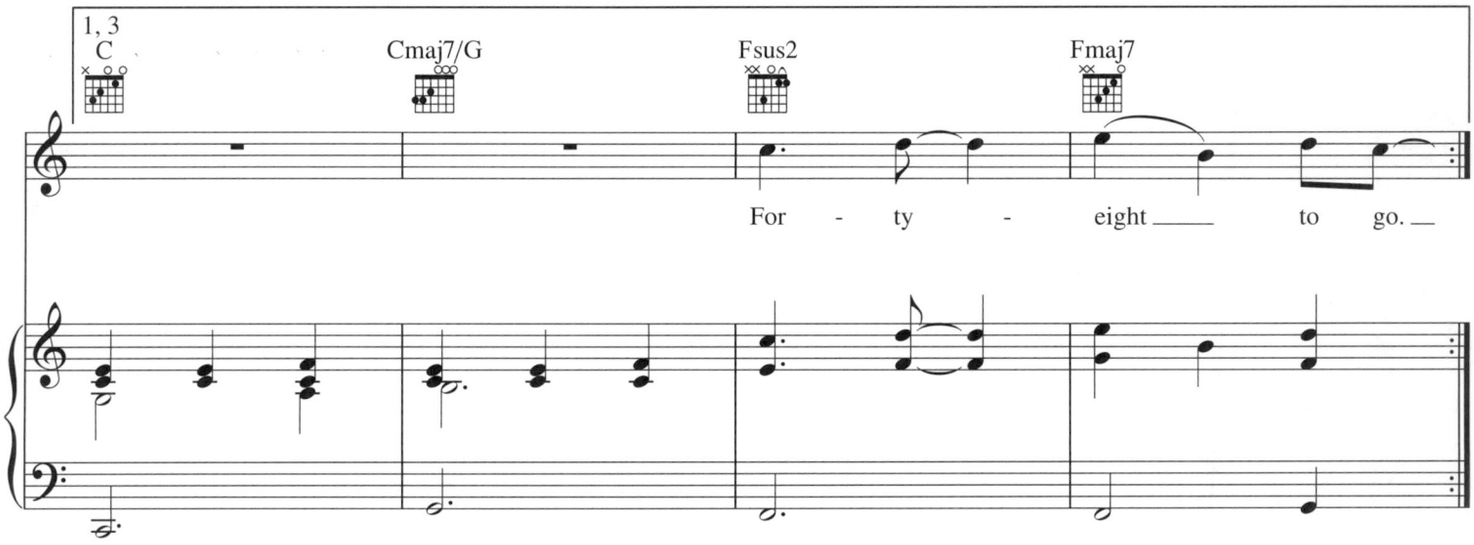
1, 3
C
Cmaj7/G
Fsus2
Fmaj7
For - ty - eight to go.

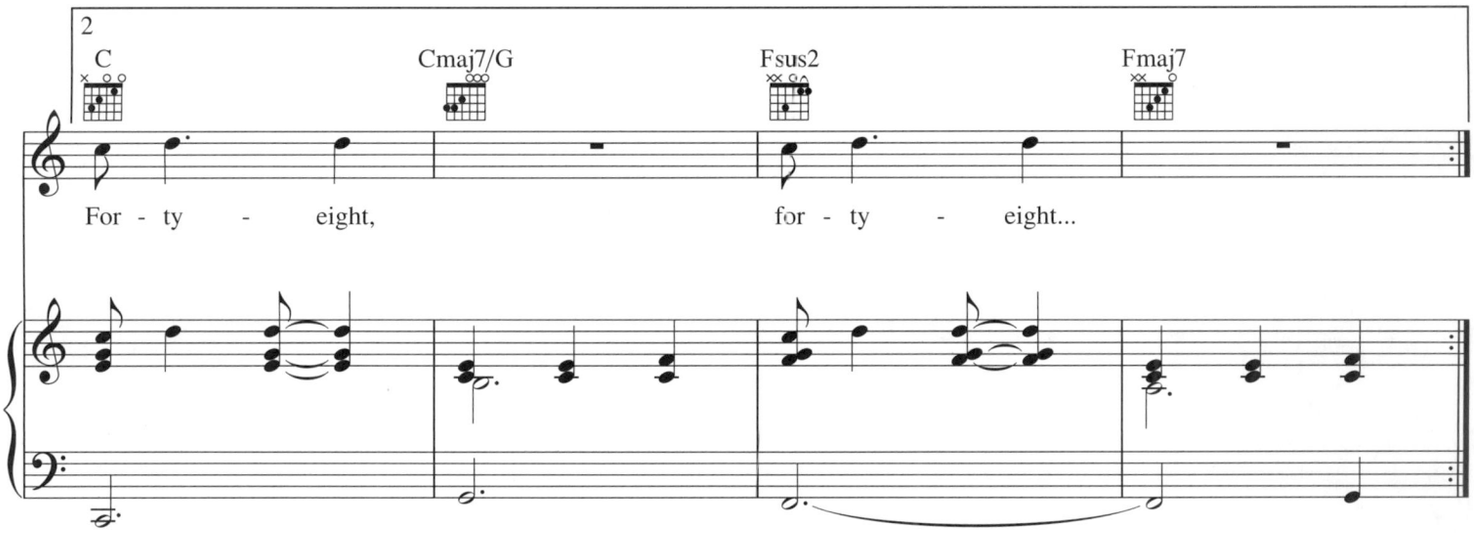
2
C
Cmaj7/G
Fsus2
Fmaj7
For - ty - eight, for - ty - eight...

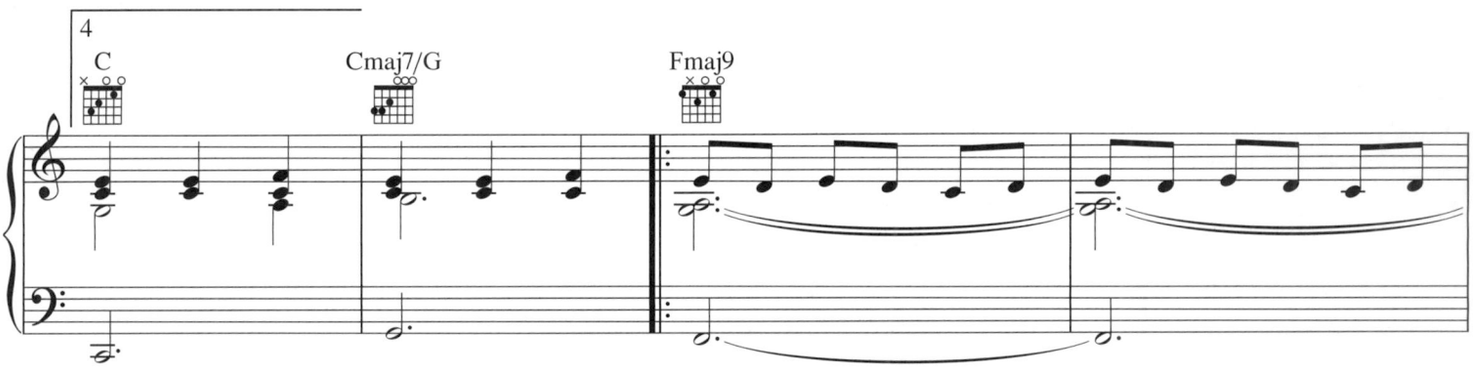
4
C
Cmaj7/G
Fmaj9

Repeat ad lib.
Final Ending
Fmaj7

RAINY ZURICH

Words and Music by JOSEPH KING
and ISAAC SLADE

* *Recorded a half step higher.*

© 2012 EMI APRIL MUSIC INC., LITTLE BIKE MUSIC and LINCOLN & OLLIE MUSIC
All Rights Controlled and Administered by EMI APRIL MUSIC INC.
All Rights Reserved International Copyright Secured Used by Permission

F
C/E
Am
Em/G
breath - ing in, you're breath - ing out the same. We give and take, and
In the home, she's in a lone - ly room with mu - sic play - ing.
F
C/E
Am
G/B
let the wat - er fall on the flame; it's not burn - ing out. I'll
Can't she hear my heart com - ing through on the door be - tween?
Dm7(add4)
3fr
C/E
F(add2)
G(add4)
Dm7(add4)
3fr
C
keep you warm, danc-ing in a down - pour. And I will hold your
Fmaj9
G(add4)
Dm7(add4)
3fr
C/E
bod - y slow - ly turn - ing. I'll keep you warm,

F(add2)
G(add4)
Dm7(add4)
3fr
C
To Coda
danc - ing n a down - pour, and breath - ing in, we'll
1
Fmaj9
G(add4)
F5
C/E
take it off and soak our skin,
Am
Gsus
3fr
F5
C/E
Am
Gsus
3fr
soak our skin.
She's
2
Fmaj9
G(add4)
G
F
take it off and soak...
May - be I'll find you;

Am
Dm/C
G
F
may - be I won't.
Ba - by, I'll try to.
Am
Dm/C
G
F
E - ven if I don't,
you are what I nev - er knew I need-
Am
Dm/C
G
F
- ed, what I nev - er knew I need - ed, what I nev - er knew I need-
F5
Am
Gsus
3fr
F5
- ed.
Al - most there.

Am
Gsus
3fr
D.S. al Coda
And I'll
CODA
Fmaj9
G(add4)
take it off and soak
Dm(add2)
5fr
C(add2)
Fmaj7
G(add4)
Dm(add2)
5fr
C(add2)
our skin, and soak our skin.
Fmaj7
G(add4)
Fmaj7
C(add2)/E
F/A
G(add4)
Ooh.
Dm(add2)
5fr
C(add2)
Fmaj7
G(add4)
N.C.

BE STILL

Words and Music by JOSEPH KING,
ISAAC SLADE, DAVID WELSH
and BEN WYSOCKI

© 2012 EMI APRIL MUSIC INC., LITTLE BIKE MUSIC, LINCOLN & OLLIE MUSIC, MOKOS MUSIC and POTALIAN PUBLISHING
All Rights for LITTLE BIKE MUSIC and LINCOLN & OLLIE MUSIC Controlled and Administered by EMI APRIL MUSIC INC.
All Rights Reserved International Copyright Secured Used by Permission

G
D/F♯
Am
Em7
still and know that I'm with you. Be
G
D7/F♯
G
still, be still and know. When
G
D7/F♯
Am
Em7
dark - ness comes up - on you and
you go through the val - ley, and the
G
D
C
Em7
cov - ers you with fear and shame, be
shad - ow comes down from the hill; if

G
D/F♯
Am
Em7
still and know that I'm with you, and I
morn - ing nev - er comes to be, be still,
G
D/F♯
G
will say your name. If
be still, be still. If
C
Em7
C
Em7
ter - ror falls up - on your bed, and
you for - get the way to go and
G
D
sleep no long - er comes, re - mem -
lose where you came from, if no

G
D/F♯
Am
Em7
- ber all the words I said; be
one is stand - ing be - side you, be
G
D/F♯
G
1
still, be still, and know. And when
still and know I am.
2
G
D/F♯
Am
Be still and know that I'm with you;
Em7
G
D/F♯
G
be still and know I am.
rit.